Selected American Game Birds

David Hagerbaumer
with
Sam Lehman

Selected American Game Birds

The Caxton Printers, Ltd.
Caldwell, Idaho.
1980

First Printing October, 1972
Second Printing May 1973
Third Printing September, 1980

International Standard Book Number 0-87004-213-0
Library of Congress Catalogue Number 74-137773

Lithographed and bound in the United States of America
by
The Caxton Printers, Ltd
Caldwell, Idaho
135876

Dedication

To the distaff side-Gladys Thagerbaumer and Edie Lehman- without whose careful assistance and suggestions this book would never have been completed.

Contents

Biography

David Hagerbaumer

The art of wildfowl painting certainly has to offer a challenge that, if pursued to its fullest, is as demanding as anything an artist can undertake. Not only a complete knowledge of an art technique itself is necessary but also a comprehensive understanding of ornithology, botany and the ecological system that ties the two together.

In my judgement, no other man has accepted this challenge with more dedication than David W. Hagerbaumer. Dave lives on an eighty acre tract of wilderness in western Oregon with his wife Gladys who, besides being his business manager, is a continual source of encouragement to him. It is difficult for me to talk about Dave alone because it is always "Dave and Gladys" who, in every phase, have undertaken this venture together.

Dave's career began along the Mississippi River bottoms near Quincy, Illinois, where he grew up. It was there that he gained a vast store of knowledge about the countless numbers of waterfowl that inhabited the area. He became an excellent wing shot but, of more significance, a very keen observer. With an early interest in drawing and painting, he was destined to become a wildlife painter.

Because of the numerous references available today on

artists both living and dead, it is quite customary for the new-comer to closely follow the style of one of his predecessors. Actually, not only is it customary but in many cases quite accept-able because, after all, how does one learn but by absorbing the knowledge pioneered by others. however, when discussing Dave's technique, it is the exception rather than the custom because he has developed a style with not only a beautiful freshness and complete authoritative quality, but one that is definitely his own.

During the Korean War he was a staff artist with the Fleet Marine Force and later attended San Diego College for three years, majoring in art education. At the end of this period he abruptly decided against a teaching profession. Probably one of the most important phases of his career was while he was the staff artist and assistant ornithologist at the Santa Barbara Museum of Natural history. he has since traveled, hunted, photographed and sketched in the areas of North America inhabited by the various species of waterfowl and upland game that he paints, assuring the complete authenticity not only in his birds but in his backgrounds as well.

Dave's related accomplishments including his outstanding bird ceramics and wood carvings are too numerous to discuss here. Of principal concern are his paintings which in my esti-mation are unparalled in his field.

David A. Maass

Biography

Sam Lehman

Henry James once said, "I live, live intensely and am fed by life, and my value, whatever it be, is my own kind of expression of that."

Sam Lehman, too, is a man who lives intensely. And his work in this volume is an expression of a full life, an observant life, reflecting a knowledge of letters, birds and art, and the discipline that allows one to master the flat-edged pen.

Mr. Lehman began studying calligraphy (literally beautiful writing) after he retired because he could not read his own hand writing. Once started, he found it to be a consuming interest that left little time for anything except family and fishing. He says, "Calligraphy is a controlled means of expressing your latent or presumed talent." As a reader can determine easily, his talent with the pen is not presumed.

In writing out the text of a book, Sam Lehman adopts a practice used throughout the history of man until the development of machines that could reproduce multiple copies. Handwriting has been on the decline since. It is a distinct pleasure to find this kind of effort, particularly when combined with the talents of David Hagerbaumer.

Mr. Lehman's writing here is not in a particular historical alphabet. It is a combination of three alphabets, with his own modi-

Sam Lehman - continued

fications. He tells us he chose these letters because they are very legible and look good on the book page. Agreed!

Sam Lehman was born in Shawnee, Oklahoma in 1899, and lived in Kansas before moving to Oregon in 1917. He concluded a long career as a banker and home loan officer with the Veterans Administration when he retired in 1963. He has always led an active life with more to do than time could accommodate. He is an accomplished craftsman with silver, wood, enamel, leather and silkscreen and is an avid gardener. He has produced more than twenty manuscript books on fishing flies, which he has illustrated with water color drawings. A hunter and fisherman since boyhood, Sam has a particular affinity for pheasants, ducks, quail and trout.

Sam's involvement with calligraphy demonstrates how retirement can be a rich and rewarding period in one's life. We shall look forward to his next book.

Lloyd J. Reynolds

Selected American Game Birds

Ruffed Grouse
Bonasa umbellus

Gray birch, an old fallen rock fence, and a brace of ruffs thundering out~ this scene could be one of many places in the north~eastern corner of our country. The ruffed is resident in all of the northern states as well as down the eastern mountain chain to Georgia. From coast to coast the growth in the habitat is somewhat varied but in a general way the wooded areas along stream courses, old orchards, woodsy edgings and abandoned farms suit this bird.

Like most gallinaceous birds, ruffed grouse spend a great share of their time on the ground. Nests are built on the ground, usually in thick cover and often close by a log or stump or a tree trunk. The birds generally roost at night in thick brush or trees but are known to dive into snow~ drifts to spend the night. It would seem the good insulating qualities of snow might be the reason for such an act.

The true "partridge" hunter places "Old Ruff" in a class by himself where grouse are concerned~ a prestige bird in every sense of the word. Ruffed Grouse have long had a sagacious reputation and this is particularly true of those birds living generation after generation in close proximity to man. It must be noted, however, that birds living out their lives in remote areas with little or no contact with humans seem to have much less fear of man.

plate 1

Wood Duck
Aix sponsa

Full morning light has not yet come to the pond in the timber as a pair of Wood ducks threads its way through the trees. Considered by many to be our most beautiful waterfowl the wood duck is indeed spectacular. Even the hen, though more somber in tones than the drake, shows more colors than other female ducks. Suited to flying among trees, these ducks have long, wide tails and big wings. This large air foil enables them to fly swiftly and gracefully through even the most dense stands of timber.

The only puddle duck that nests in trees, the woodie chooses a hollow trunk or limb. An opening into a cavity of barely four inches in diameter is sufficient for the hen to enter. The young leave the nest by jumping to the ground or water below on command from the mother a very short time after hatching.

Favored haunts are fresh water ponds and marshy pools within a wooded area. It is here they find food, shelter and nesting sites. Acorns are a prized food of wood ducks.

Our prairie states have a much smaller wood duck population than the eastern third of the nation or the west coast. They winter mainly in the southern states on inland fresh waters within woods.

This species responds well to management. Areas with few natural nesting cavities left, can, with the placement of nest boxes in trees along streams and pond edges, build up wood duck numbers. Sensible regulations and nest box programs in every state have brought about a favorable comeback from lows of forty years ago. The wood duck population looks good at this time.

plate 2

Common Goldeneye and Barrow's Goldeneye
Bucephala clangula   Bucephala islandica

Winter has come to a marsh on the Great Lakes. Driving downwind through the falling snow hurtles a flock of whistlers. Cold weather holds no fear for these birds for they will hang around as long as there is open water.

The Common Goldeneye is found in limited measure throughout the entire country while the Barrow's is most numerous in the west and to some extent in the far northeast.

Goldeneyes are divers of extreme hardiness. In flight their wings produce an unusually loud, far reaching whistling sound, hence their most common colloquial name~ whistlers.

The drake Barrow's is identified by his crescent shaped face patch and the drake Common by his round patch. For the average person identifying the females as Barrow's or Common is next to impossible. These divers are tree nesters - often near high mountain streams. Unlike some species of diving ducks, goldeneyes are most likely to be seen in small groups rather than in large rafts. Whistlers are more wary than most divers and do not decoy with the usual abandon.

Goldeneyes bring to mind cold weather, storms, white caps and floating ice, blowing snow and freezing spray. In short, these are the ducks that fit perfectly into the type of day most waterfowlers hope for. Whether you meet this duck tending her brood on a mountain stream in the Rockies of Wyoming, on a sunny November afternoon along the Columbia River or over decoys in a driving gale on Lake Superior, they are still the same bird~ big, strong and hardy.

plate 3

Common Snipe
Capella gallinago delicata

With twisting, dodging flight a snipe comes into its favorite habitat~ an open boggy meadow or marsh.

Common snipe have feeding habits much like those of the woodcock although the snipe prefers a more open situation. The bills of the two are similar~adapted to the capture of their favorite food~ earthworms. Snipe are solitary birds and while they are often found in concentrations on favored feeding grounds they tend to travel alone. Unlike members of the same family (Scolopacidae) the sandpipers, they do not share the flocking habit.

The courtship flight of the male snipe is a delightful performance. Flying high in the air the bird suddenly sets his wings and with tail spread wide, pitches downward. It is believed that the air rushing by the stiff outer tail feathers produces a lovely mellow whistling, a sound not unlike the soft call of the screech owl.

Snipe breed in northern latitudes from ocean to ocean but as fall approaches, the southerly migration begins. Most snipe winter in the moderate climates as freezing temperatures will render the bulk of their feeding grounds useless. A few snipe will winter in areas that have freezing weather, seeking out small areas that do not freeze solidly, around springs and along banks of flowing streams.

Jack snipe, as they were once called, have long been a much favored game bird from coast to coast, though not sought by the great numbers of hunters as are such species as bobwhite and dove.

Like woodcock coverts, that may be void of birds one day and loaded the next, snipe bogs and meadows are the same. Migrating birds will often fill an area overnight and leave it empty just as suddenly. They are one of our truly classic game birds.

plate 4

Redhead
Aythya americana

Redheads on a Texas tidal marsh are a common sight from Matagordo Bay to the Rio Grande during the fall and winter months. More than half of all American redheads winter in the Laguna Madre area of Texas and Mexico. Other important wintering grounds lie in the middle Atlantic seaboard and the coastal area of western Mexico.

Nesting farther south than many species, goodly numbers of redheads are reared annually in the continental United States mainly in the west where some deep water marsh acreage still remains.

In years past, redheads ranked second only to the canvasbacks in importance as a market species. A famous area in the old days was the Chesapeake Bay region where the standard method of gunning the divers was from sink boxes or battery and offshore stake blinds. Most redheads are bagged incidentally along with a mixed bag of other species. There are still a few places left, however, where a man can, by putting forth the effort and with the correct rig, nearly duplicate an old time redhead hunt. He must be willing to accept a small limit, and be thankful that such a hunt can still be had at all.

Redheads are fine table ducks. Though slightly smaller than the famed canvasback, it may be difficult indeed to distinguish between the two in flavor. Tradition will, however, probably rule in favor of the canvasback.

plate 5

Greater Scaup and Lesser Scaup
Aythya marila   Aythya affinis

Morning fog clings to the water of an abandoned log pond on the central Oregon coast. Into the scene comes a mixed flock of bluebills-common winter residents of this area, often known as broadbills and blackheads.

The Greater scaup tends to be more of a coastal bird than the Lesser, common to inland fresh waters. A notable exception is the tremendous concentration of wintering Lesser scaup on the coast of Texas. Both species are found together to some extent throughout the entire country.

In flight the two species are difficult to tell apart. In the hand the purplish head of the drake Lesser will distinguish it from the drake Greater scaup with its greenish head sheen. The white on the wings of the hen is one key to species. The hen Lesser has white only on the wing speculum while on the Greater the white extends out into several of the primary feathers.

To the hunter, who favors divers, the scaup today makes up the bulk of the bag. Their populations are holding up well, and in some cases increasing in such numbers that they are classed as bonus birds. Both species are "raft ducks", tending to gang up on both feeding and nesting waters.

While broadbills may lack some of the glamour of canvasbacks in the minds of the old timers, at present there are many waterfowlers who would never know diver gunning were it not for the more plentiful scaup. Like all divers, their flight is rapid and direct.

As table fare, scaup can be very good or very bad. As game birds, they are always great.

plate 6

Bobwhite Quail
Colinus virginianus

A covey of bobwhites flushes from the grasses beneath the pines in the southeast. This is the setting for what most hunters would specify as traditional quail country.

The bobwhite is the most famous of our quail and occupies the largest range. While found in the greatest numbers in our southern tier of states, they do occur as far north as Wyoming, South Dakota and Minnesota. Bobwhite have been introduced into the far west and northwest but the transplants have not been too successful.

The finest bobwhite habitat is found in the south-eastern Atlantic and Gulf states including Texas. A large portion of the finest bobwhite cover in these states is the "piney woods" type. Grass, brushy edgings, cultivated fields within the pine woods is the picture most people recall when bobwhite are mentioned. Other fine bobwhite country, south Texas for example, may not look a bit like the classic "piney woods" but contains great bobwhite concentrations.

Bobwhite nest and roost on the ground. Good sized clutches are the rule with twelve to fifteen eggs as an average. They have a habit of roosting in a circle, especially in cold weather, with heads out and bodies touching.

Hunting bobwhites has been a sport for both man and dog. Pointers and setters both are used. Generally, in times past, the gunners followed the dogs in horse or mule drawn wagons, more recently, in four wheel drive vehicles. When the dogs make game, the gunners dismount and walk up to the dogs on point. Dogs cover so much territory seeking game it is a must for hunters to have some mode of transport other than on foot. Bobwhite is probably our most popular and widely known game bird.

plate 7

Canada Goose
Branta canadensis

A dozen honkers, on set wings, lower majestically for a landing on calm waters of a Hatteras marsh.

The Canada is the best known of all our geese and easily identified by the black head and neck and white cheek patch. More than a dozen sub-species are recognized today which range in size from the mallard-sized cackling goose to the nearly swan-sized Giant long believed to be extinct. All, however, have the black head and neck and white cheek patch. Body coloration varies somewhat in the various sub-species but generally is grey-brown.

Canada geese always have had the reputation for wariness. This is indeed true in the case of the larger races where they are heavily hunted.

Honkers have set patterns of feeding and resting. Careful study of these patterns is necessary for the goose hunter to have consistent success in bagging these birds.

They are field feeders and will travel long distances to reach a favorite field of stubble or graze. Many goose hunters prefer to seek these geese there, hunting from pit blinds.

Some of the larger wintering concentrations of Canada geese are on the Eastern Seaboard; Horicon Marsh National Wildlife Refuge, in Wisconsin; Crab Orchard National Wildlife Refuge, Illinois and the Sacramento Valley in California.

Canada geese are more successfully managed than most waterfowl. Consequently these geese are now observed in places never seen before and in areas from which they had formerly been driven.

plate 8

Lesser Snow Goose
Chen hyperborea hyperborea

Blue Goose
Chen caerulescens

As a flock of snow geese sweeps by overhead, noticeable among the white birds are several dark individuals. Most of these dark birds are blue geese plus one immature snow goose.

Blue geese are a color phase of the snow geese and steadily increasing in proportion of blues to snows. The blue phase is in the majority in south-eastern Louisiana while in the rice fields of Texas around Eagle Lake, the blues make up only about twenty-five per-cent of the wintering flocks. The blue is a rare bird on the Pacific wintering areas at this time.

Greater snow geese winter on the Atlantic coast and have no blue phase. The lesser snow goose is a bird of the West with the larger concentrations on the Gulf Coast and the interior valleys of California. Puget Sound also has a wintering flock of considerable size.

Snow geese are far northern nesters and, unlike many waterfowl, nest in dense concentrations. Over one thousand pairs to the square mile have been recorded.

Snows and blues are hunted usually over decoy spreads in har-vested grain fields, the rice stubble of the Sacramento valley and Eagle Lake being a couple of the best areas. The Louisiana coast is another favorite.

Certainly a greater variety of objects is used to decoy snow geese than any other goose. In the fields of the areas hunted can be seen scattered about the blinds such objects as paper plates, sheets of news-paper, pieces of white cloth, bakery sacks as well as the conven-ional full bodied and silhouette field decoys, both homemade and manufactured.

plate 9

California Quail
Lophortyx californicus

From a grassy, cactus studded hillside on the east slope of the coast range in central California, a small covey of quail explodes in flight. Here among the digger pines of the canyon slopes the California quail is at home.

A number of subspecies of this bird occur in other types of habitat from Washington on into Mexico.

In California these quail are usually called Valley quail, their most common colloquial name. Unlike the bobwhite, the California is, as a rule, a bird of large coveys and in the old days coveys of several hundred birds were not uncommon.

Valley quail live only in the states of the far west and Mexico. They are the most important quail of this region from the gunner's point of view. Hunting them can be a much different experience from hunting the bobwhite. While dogs are used on Valley quail, they are not considered so much of a standard part of the hunt as for bobwhite. Most good California quail coverts are thicker than typical bobwhite cover. More often than not they include cactus and/or thorned wild berry patches. Not often are these western quail discovered in open grassy areas.

California quail are one of three plumed quail whose principal home is the western United States. The other two are the Gambel's, a desert species, and the mountain-the largest of our quail-found only in the mountains and foothills of the far west ranges.

plate 10

American Widgeon
Mareca americana

With the soft, mellow whistling calls of the drakes settling over the marshy edge of a Cascade lake, a flock of widgeon drop down steeply for a landing. These birds are on migration and eventually, after resting, will go on to seek winter quarters in the Sacramento or Imperial valleys of California or on a marsh in the vastness of Mexico's high interior.

Until recently, this bird was commonly called baldpate so it is with difficulty that many old-timers remember them as widgeon.

A puddle duck, like the mallard and teal, the widgeon feeds in the shallows of marshes and rivers and in fields where they graze on greens to a much greater extent than do other ducks. Widgeon are graceful as they walk. That characteristic coupled with their short bills causes them to resemble small geese as they wander about grazing.

American widgeon are very common and seem to have had more success than many other species in withstanding the inroads of civilization. A new world duck, they are found throughout the United States. North America is their only breeding place.

Widgeon are great game birds. They decoy well and are fancy fliers. Usually their flocks occur as a dense mass of birds, often of great size. They make no apparent effort to form or hold ranks or lines. During migration on the Pacific flyway flocks of widgeon numbering a hundred birds or more decoy as readily as do those that fly singly.

plate 11

American Brant
Branta bernicla hrota

It is winter on the Jersey shore. A weak, cold sun struggles through the overcast. The pale light is reflected on the chop of the bay water and fishing shacks out on the strand are silhouetted in the sun's track~a typical scene on much of the Atlantic coast during this time of year. To complete the picture are the flighting brant~a common winter resident from New Jersey to the Carolinas.

With the brant hunting fraternity there is no goose to match this one. Brant are true sea geese and rarely is a specimen found away from salt water. On both the Atlantic and Pacific coasts brant feed mainly on eelgrass which they seek out on the ebb tides.

American brant are found on the Atlantic coast while Black brant are confined to the Pacific. The difference in the two is only one of coloration, with the Pacific species being darker on flanks and breasts. Though small for geese, about the size in body of large mallards, but with long, pointed wings, they do appear much larger.

On the Atlantic, areas like Barnegat, Monomoy and Ocra~coke stir the brant hunter's enthusiasm while on the Pacific side Tillamook, Netarts, Humboldt and San Quintin are some of the most important bays. Fine brant wintering areas are disappearing~San Diego Bay and Mission Bay to name two. Perhaps the few remaining can somehow be retained.

plate 12

Ring-Necked Pheasant
Phasianus colchicus

With much cackling and thunder of wings, a trio of pheasants erupt from a grassy swale. It was here on Petersen Butte, Linn County, Oregon in 1882 that the first Ring-Necks were released. Today this bird- as a result of repeated plantings-has dispersed into virtually every state of the land. Many areas have been more to his liking than his first home, the mid-Willamette valley of Oregon. Some notable spots are the Dakotas, Nebraska, Southern Minnesota, also Pelee Island, the Palouse region of Washington and the Sacramento Valley.

Certainly the pheasant is one of our most popular upland game birds. Big and gaudy, the Ring-Neck is eagerly sought by shooters wherever he has chosen to live.

Because pheasants can be so successfully reared on game farms, they are popular for plantings in covers for a "put and take" type of hunting. The majority of our states now engage in a pheasant rearing program of some sort. The Ring-Neck is, in addition, the most utilized species on the more recently popular "pay as you shoot" hunting clubs.

Being gallinaceous birds, pheasant are ground nesters and dwellers. In the United States they occupy a variety of habitat ranging from irrigated lands in the deserts to the regions in which they do best- the diversified farming areas of the Dakotas and Nebraska.

Ring-Neck populations tend to fluctuate from year to year. Weather, disease and changes in agricultural practices may all be factors in these ups and downs.

plate 13

Pintail
Anas acuta

Over the fog shrouded marsh a quartet of pintails loafs along. Our most widely distributed duck and almost as well known as the mallard, the pintail is easily recognized in any plumage by its long, graceful silhouette. Called sprig throughout much of the west, the pintail is most abundant in the western two-thirds of the country.

A puddle duck, like the mallard and teal, pintails prefer a habitat of large open marsh with shallow water and short growth. This duck has also learned to utilize the cultivated lands and on wintering grounds, use fields planted to wheat, barley, rice and millet. They can be found wintering on salt water as well as fresh.

As a game species, the sprig ranks with the canvasback and the mallard. Wherever encountered, pintails will prove to be wary birds and a prize on both the marsh and the table.

Some famous pintail spots in the United States are Sacramento Valley, Salton Sea, Gulf Coast, Bear River Marsh, and the Tule Lake-Lower Klamath area.

Sprig are hunted in most places over decoys. It should always be remembered that in gunning this species, they lack tolerance for the closed-in wooded areas so favored by mallards and wood ducks. The most carefully placed spread of fine decoys will usually do little good in attracting the pintail unless rigged in an open marsh area. At times sprig respond to a well used whistle call.

To the water fowler of the west the sprig is king of puddle ducks.

plate 14

Canvasback
Aythya valisineria

With a rush of air over set pinions, Canvasbacks drive downwind over bending marsh grasses. To many, this scene would be the ultimate in waterfowling as the canvasback is considered by a majority of bird hunters to be the king of ducks. The "can" is a North American species, infrequently a straggler in ranges beyond.

Divers, the canvasbacks prefer large open bodies of water both fresh and saline. Famous wintering areas are Chesapeake Bay, the Gulf Coast and San Pablo Bay as well as some high lakes in Mexico.

They feed heavily on vegetable matter, obtained mainly by diving. Eastern "cans" have long had the reputation for excellence as a table bird presumably since their favored food is wild celery (vallisneria).

In the old days when market gunning was in full swing, the canvasback was the mainstay of the trade. On east coast wintering areas the majority of the birds were shot from batteries. Large stools of decoys were employed in conjunction with sink boxes. Daily bags of ducks that numbered in the hundreds were recorded. The battery and sink box were outlawed many years ago. One of the most famous regions of all time for this type of waterfowling was the Susquehanna Flats on upper Chesapeake Bay.

Due mainly to drainage of breeding grounds, the Canvasbacks have been harder hit than many of our other species of ducks. Klamath and Malheur Lakes and marshes in Oregon still produce a few birds but for the most part the few remaining Canvasbacks breed in Canada and Alaska.

plate 15

Band-Tailed Pigeon
Columba fasciata

A misty rain falls over the Oregon Cascades as scattered flocks of wild pigeons drift across a burned-over ridge, headed perhaps for some mineral spring or favored feeding area.

This pigeon of the west ranges from Canada to Nicaragua and as far eastward as Utah and Colorado. They average in size about the same as our domestic pigeon of the barnyard and city street. (Rock dove- Columba livia).

Generally the diet of the band-tail is vegetable but will, of course, vary with the area. Acorns, elder-berries and cultivated grain are some of the favored foods.

They are tree nesters and like most of their kind build a loose platform-like structure of twigs and lay, usually, one or rarely two eggs. Band-Tails are not colony nesters as were the Passenger pigeons.

As a game bird, the Band-Tail is not as well known as many of our game bird species, undoubtedly because of its restricted range of the far west. Popular and most productive hunting spots are often at natural mineral springs. The birds have watered at these springs for countless generations but why they are so sought out is not exactly known. Other areas to hunt are crossing points on mountain ridges used on watering and feeding flights.

Band-Tails are capable of dazzling flight speeds and for the wing shot, are unquestionably one of the most challenging of our game birds.

plate 16

White-fronted Goose
Anser albifrons frontalis

It is warm this November afternoon on a marsh in California's central valley. To the east, the Marysville Buttes rise boldly from the valley floor while, beyond, the Sierra Nevadas stand tall and mighty in dim relief. Then from the north come the laughing calls of a small flock of specklebellies. Eagerly they lose altitude and prepare to land. Their flight from the arctic nesting grounds has been a long one and it is here they will spend the winter and spring, in sunny California.

Call him specklebelly, speck, or laughing goose - all these colloquial names will identify this bird in the west as the white-fronted goose. "Specks" are found mostly west of the Mississippi. Main wintering areas are the Sacramento Valley of California, the coastal plains of Texas, western Louisiana and Mexico.

Like most geese, the white-front is a grazer but will also, on occasion, feed in the stubble. Wintering, too, in the central valley of California and in Mexico is a subspecies called the Tule White-fronted goose that remains something of a mystery. It is a little larger and generally darker in coloration and the breeding grounds are not known. There seem to be but a few of these birds left on these wintering grounds and some fear is being voiced as to their future. Let us hope that enough of their life history can be learned to allow management practices to be enacted to secure the future of this subspecies -- in time.

plate 17

Blue-Winged Teal
Anas discors

Fall has barely arrived. Few if any leaves have fallen and already the blue-wings are well down the Mississippi on their southerly migration. A "warm weather" duck-in a hurry to get to the Gulf Coast and beyond for the winter-is reluctant to head north again in the spring until all threat of bad weather has passed. This is the blue-wing.

A small duck, only slightly larger than the green-winged teal, the blue-wing is a bird that favors a fresh-water habitat, seldom using saline areas. A dabbling duck, this species finds its food in shallow ponds, sloughs and marshes. Fond of grain, like many others, it will also be found, at times, in stubble fields.

This bird winters farther south than most of our ducks. While a good number spend the winter on the marshes of the gulf states, many more go on to Mexico, Central America and even South America. They are also found wintering on many of the Bahama islands. Blue-wing have long been held in great favor with waterfowlers. Not only do they decoy readily but like all teal are fast and erratic flyers and most delicious table fare. Found mainly in the Mississippi and Central flyways, it seldom reaches the Pacific Coast. A few are found in such western areas as the Malheur and Klamath basins of Oregon but in such small numbers that to see one is an event. Like the blue-wings elsewhere, these, too, migrate so early that many waterfowlers in the far west do not know them.

plate 18

Turkey
Meleagris gallopavo

Moving cautiously through the oaks and cactus in the hill country of Texas is the largest of our upland game birds. The turkeys' principal homes are in the southwest, the Gulf states, the Carolinas and north through Arkansas, Missouri and eastward into Pennsylvania. Some years ago, our several races of wild turkey had all but disappeared from much of their original range. Through re-introduction a great share of this habitat has been populated once again. In fact, in many areas that never before had wild turkey, they can now be found.

The several races of turkey here live in surroundings as varied as one can imagine. One likes the warm, humid sea level environment of Florida, while another of the far Southwest is native to the pine forests where they often winter above elevations of 7000 feet in deep snow conditions. Another race is native to the hardwood forests of mid-America and northeastward into the mountains of Pennsylvania. The Rio Grande turkey, pictured here, is indigenous to much of Texas.

It is generally agreed that wild turkeys are among our more wary game birds. Methods of hunting vary but the most common is that of hunting from a blind and calling the birds into range. In some states it is legal to hunt them with either shotgun or rifle and in some places the rifle is probably the more efficient.

Wild and domestic birds are much alike~the major difference being the shape. The wild bird presents a slender, streamlined silhouette while the domestic turkey is heavy, husky in body and head. Adult wild toms may go to twenty-five pounds but average far less. Because domestic and wild birds cross readily, keeping wild strains pure in some areas may present a problem.

plate 19

Clapper Rail
Rallus longirostris crepitans

It is a balmy fall afternoon and there is a flood tide in the salt marsh on the middle Atlantic shore. Suddenly ahead of the poled boat a pair of Clapper rail takes flight. This is the moment the true "rail bird" gunner dreams of.

Living in a habitat ill-suited to man afoot, these birds are hunted from a boat on very high tides. These tides put enough water for travel in those areas inhabited by rail, but usually too thick to traverse by boat. A light wooden punt boat is commonly used for rail hunting. The pusher stands on a platform in the stern of the boat and the gunner sits or stands about amidships. As the boat is poled through the flooded marsh growth, the gunner remains at the ready for the flush of a bird. A large share of rail hunters hires a pusher and his boat for a "tide" just as in days past. Other species of rail are also hunted in this same manner, but usually on fresh or brackish water.

Clappers are also found on the Pacific Coast but are little sought after there, because the west coast lacks areas of the classic salt marsh habitat so suited to the pursuit of these birds by poled boat.

Each season finds fewer acres of good rail habitat as drainage of wetlands and other reclamation projects take their toll. The rail, unlike some bird species that can adapt to change, has no tolerance for a foreign habitat.

It is probable that fewer people engage in rail hunting than for any other species of game bird.

plate 20

David Hagerbaumer

Green-Winged Teal
Anas carolinensis

A small flock of ducks dashes by twisting and turning as they lose altitude for a landing on a small timber pond below. Their swift, erratic flight and small size identify them at once as teal.

The smallest of all our ducks and also one of the hardiest is the Green-Winged Teal. Unlike our other teal, this species scoffs at cold weather and is one of the earliest migrants to the northern breeding grounds. Green-Wings are known to winter as far north as British Columbia and Nova Scotia. In fact, like the mallard, this tiny duck will stay in the north as long as there are open water and food. They are among the most common species in all four of our major flyways.

Tales of outlandish speeds attained by this bird are pure fiction. Because of its small size and often helter-skelter flight patterns the speed appears to exceed that of other ducks. However, in company with other species, all exerting maximum effort to escape, in flight, their speeds seem about equal.

Being a puddle duck, the Green-Winged Teal prefers a habitat of sloughs, marshes and slow moving streams. It feeds like others of its kind by tipping up and principally on vegetable matter. While found mostly on fresh water, this teal flourishes also on the salt marshes of our coasts.

As game birds they have always been held in the highest esteem. They decoy readily and, like all teal, they are a most sporting target. Of all the ducks there is no finer table bird.

In hunting Green-Wings, whether you be shooting over mallard, widgeon or pintail decoys, seems to matter little to Green-Wings. They will decoy to all with the same recklessness.

plate 21

Mallard
Anas platyrhynchos

Winter fog swirls around the pin oaks back in the bottoms of a Mississippi flyway river. Out from the shelter of a grassy bank explodes a pair of mallards - the hen's quack of alarm ringing through the quiet timber. This is mallard country. Found in most of the Northern hemisphere, the mallard is undoubtedly the best known of all ducks. In the United States it is found in every state, more commonly in the western two-thirds.

Mallards are largely prairie nesters and the bulk of our birds now come from the central and western provinces of Canada. Being hardy birds, they are late in leaving the nesting grounds in the fall, some only when the last remaining waters freeze.

Adaptable birds, mallards have time and again proved their ability to take advantage of changes. A prime example is the Columbia Basin project in the far west with more than a million acres of irrigated cropland. Within the area mallard populations went from onehalf million birds in 1950 to about two million in 1960. It is believed that these are new birds, not attracted from other areas. Yet, adaptable as the mallard is, even this hardy species cannot cope with the drainage of breeding areas - an all too common practice at present.

Without question mallards are one of the most sought after ducks by hunters. They are not only large and showy but respond better than most ducks to good calling and decoys. In fact, many decoy readily in spite of the hunter's calling.

plate 22

Blue Grouse
Dendragapus obscurus

From among the fir branches overhead a pair of heavy bodied grouse burst forth. These are Blues~birds of the mountainous far west.

Blue grouse spend winters in the fir and spruce groves at elevations of over ten thousand feet. They live during this period entirely in the trees, feeding on the needles. In spring the migration is to somewhat lower elevations where nesting takes place on the ground. Much time is spent there during the summer months. Berries and insects form a large part of the diet while the young are being raised.

As a game bird the Blue is only locally important. Their range is the far west, and they prefer the remote mountain regions. For these reasons not a large number of hunters seek this bird. Dogs are not as commonly used in hunting Blues as for Ruffed grouse. In places where the grouse and deer seasons overlap, Blue grouse are often used as camp meat.

Most prime Blue grouse habitat is far removed from civilization so a hunt for this bird takes one into some wild and beautiful country. In the most isolated areas this bird shows little fear of man, hence is frequently called "fool hen" because of his trusting nature. However, in more heavily hunted localities this same bird is as wary as the Ruffed grouse.

plate 23

Black Duck
Anas rubripes

Flush them from a grass bordered pond in the pine barrens of Long Island or watch them decoy at dusk on an Ohio marsh and you will be seeing the duck that many waterfowlers consider the wariest of them all. Some call him black mallard or dusky mallard because in size, shape and voice blacks and mallards are alike- coloration being the principal difference. The black duck is common in the eastern third of the United States but few have been recorded from the far west. In coastal areas black ducks use salt water marsh and the open ocean readily- a trait which the mallard does not share. In inland waters their feeding habits are much alike.

Black ducks are hardy souls, the only dabblers to remain in goodly numbers during the winter on the north Atlantic coast. Some winter as far north as open water will allow and retreat southward only during severe blizzard conditions.

For years a controversy has raged on the question of separating the black duck into two subspecies, the common and the red-legged. It is doubtful that this controversy will ever entirely cease, if for no other reason than that of providing an interesting and entertaining way of spending at least part of an evening before the fire after a hard, cold day on the marsh.

plate 24

Eastern Mourning Dove
Zenaidura macroura carolinensis

In the late afternoon in the Carolinas the doves start passing through the pines on their way to water and then to roost. Protected as a song bird in some states and hunted as game birds in others the mourning dove is found in every state in the Union. The Western mourning dove differs from the Eastern only in its paler coloration. In states where doves have been hunted as a game bird for years, good management practices have proved that a sensible harvest in no way endangers the species.

During a good part of the winter doves tend to remain in flocks but as the nesting season nears they separate into pairs to nest in scattered fashion. There are those who feel that this very trait is the one to which the dove owes his very great numbers, perhaps even his actual existence, since his other habits are much the same as were those of the now extinct passenger pigeon. Nesting in colonies was one habit which made pigeons subject to wholesale slaughter.

Mourning doves are for the most part seedeaters. At certain seasons in some areas they consume great quantities of grain but a large part of their diet consists of weed seeds. The young are fed a combination of seeds and insects. In some southern areas doves raise as many as three broods each season. As a game bird the dove ranks near the top and the number harvested nationwide far exceeds any other game bird.

plate 25